Tribal Spirits

A COLLECTION OF
NATIVE AMERICAN INSPIRED ART

BY JO WALSH

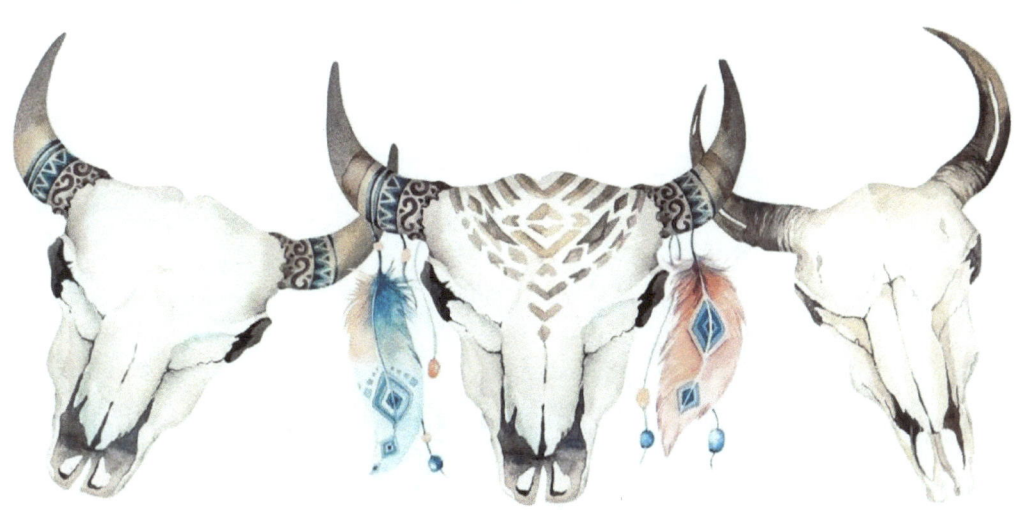

First Printing, 2019

ISBN 9781091989238

One Feather Publishing
5 Wheatlands, Ilkley
West Yorkshire, LS29 8JH
United Kingdom

www.tribalspiritsart.com

www.facebook.com/tribalspiritsart

Dedicated to
Anna & Noah
&
the many First Nations People
murdered, disenfranchised, stolen from
& dispossessed over the last several centuries

xxx

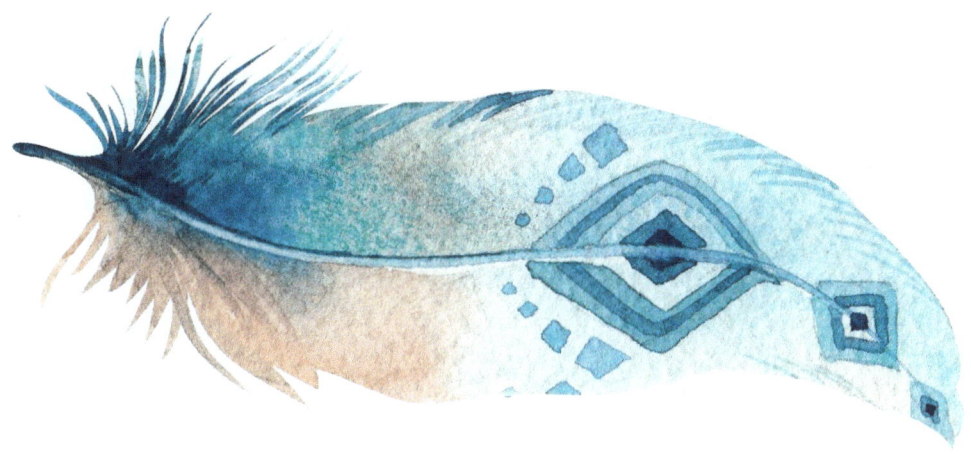

To the reader

Welcome to my very first book! I am Jo Walsh, a digital and mixed media artist with a love of dark fantasy, Gothic, surreal art and photography. I have recently become very interested in the past and present lives and culture of the Indigenous American Peoples and am currently creating a body of work inspired by them. I am researching the history of the First Nations People and the terrible way they have been, and still are, treated. I am particularly interested in their belief systems and being one with nature, Mother earth and spirit. As a consequence of this I now have a diploma in the Akashic Records from the International Alliance of Holistic Therapies and am in the process of learning about Spirit Guides.

I love to work in all kinds of media such as watercolour, pastels, collage and clay. I have taught myself to use Photoshop and enjoy bringing my art and photography into the programme to create something new and exciting. Much of my Tribal Spirits artwork is created in this way, using vintage, out of copyright photographs from the late 1800's. I feel that I am helping to bring these records of past lives back to life and I hope you find something to interest and excite you in my art as much as I have found in creating it.

Jo Walsh

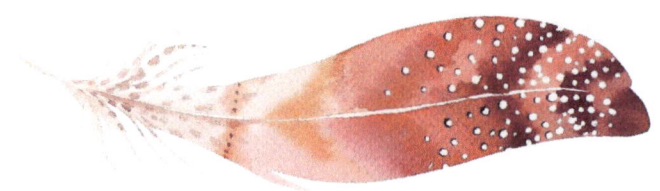

Many of the following artworks have been created using original, out of copyright, vintage photographs of the First Nations People. I have tried to be as accurate as possible naming them and/or their tribal connections, correctly. If I have made any glaring errors please accept my apologies and feel free to update me at jo@tribalspiritsart.com

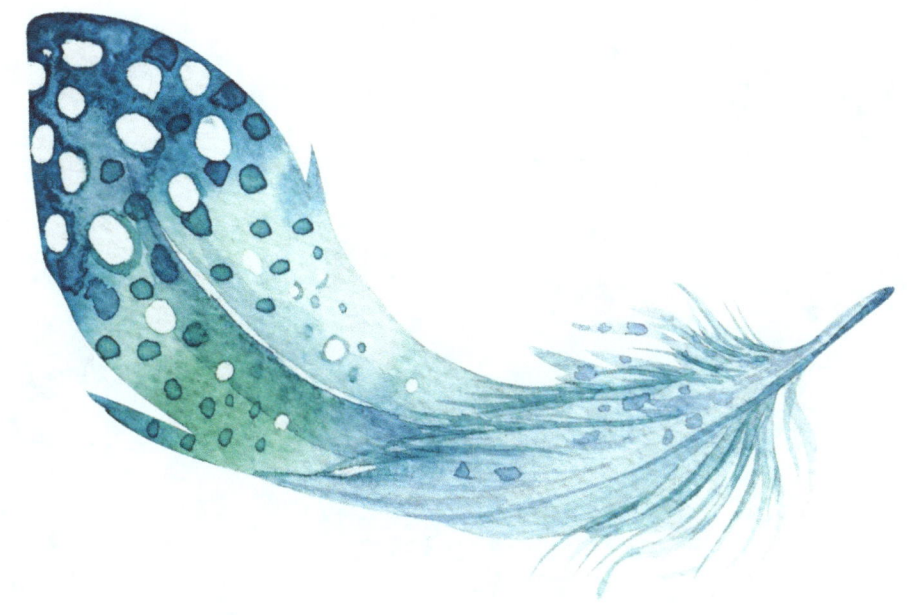

Two Whistles

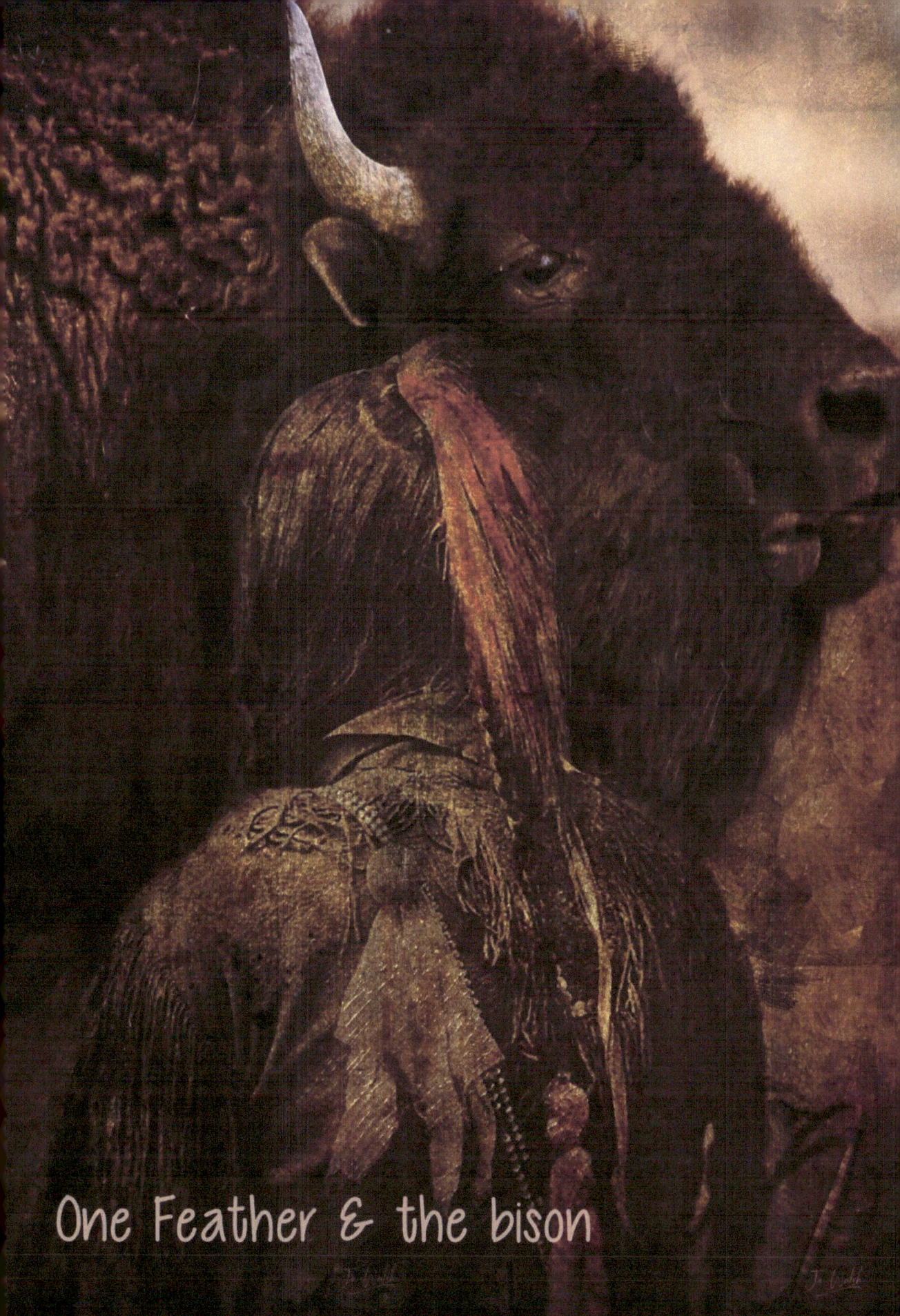

One Feather & the bison

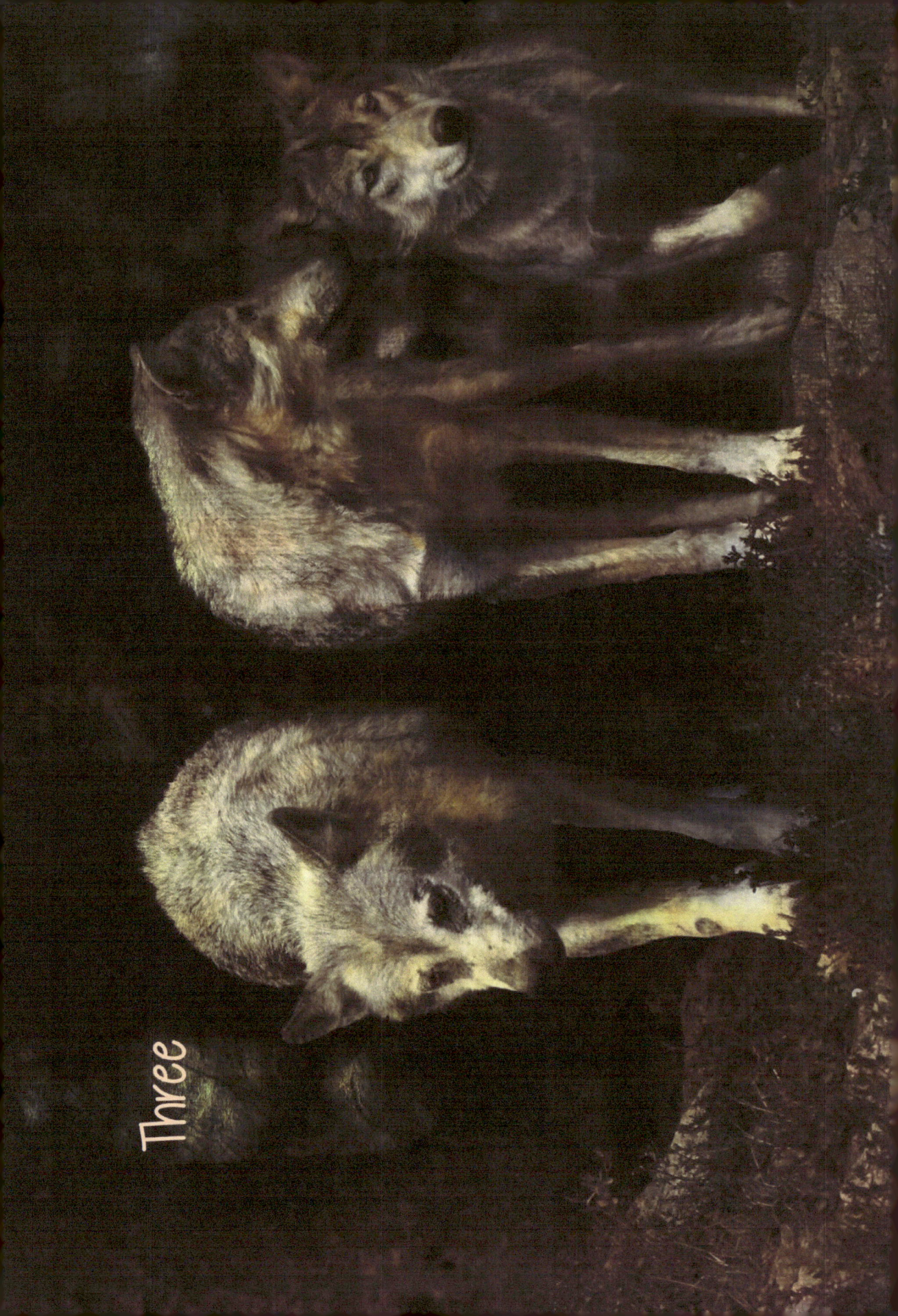

Three

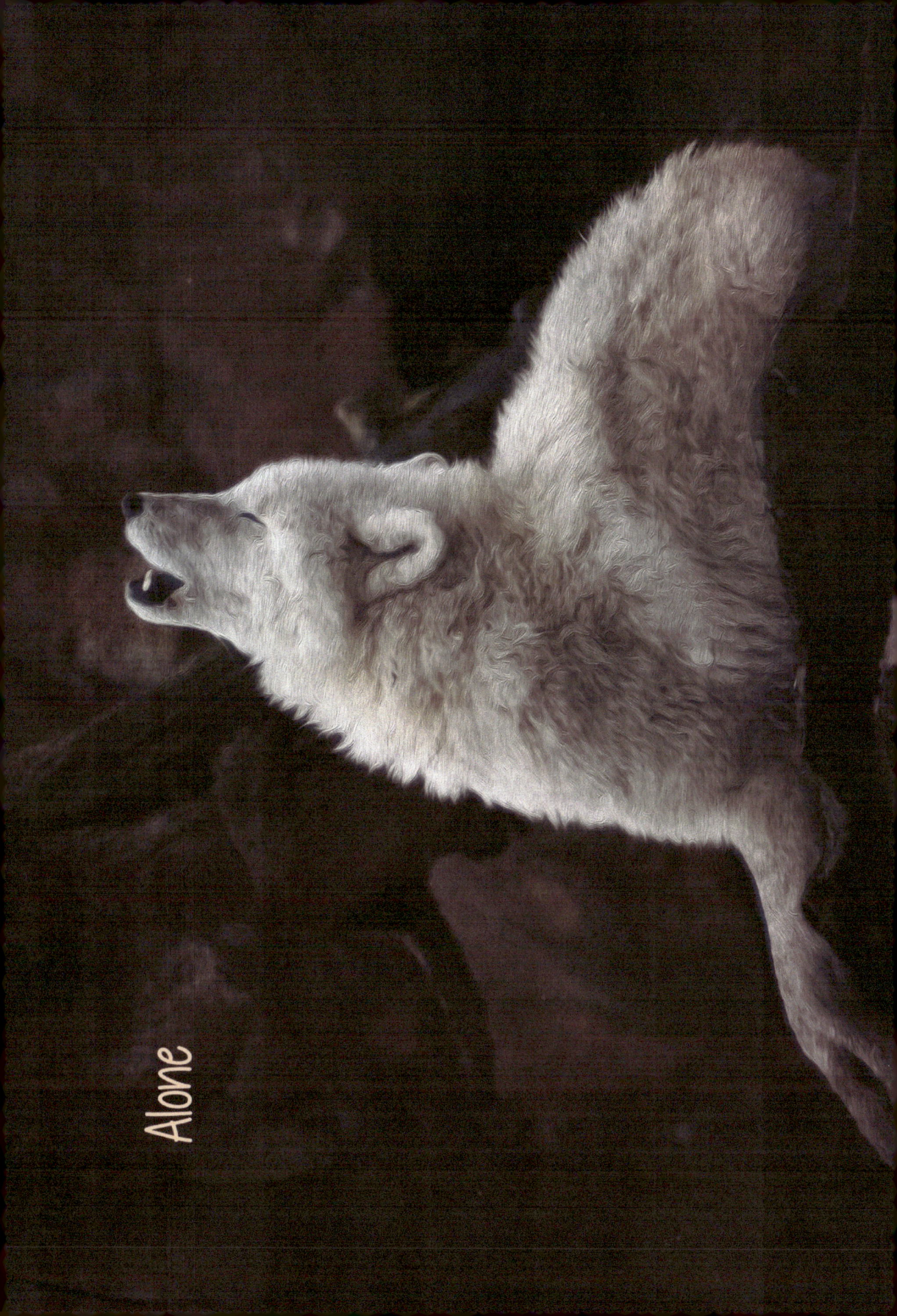

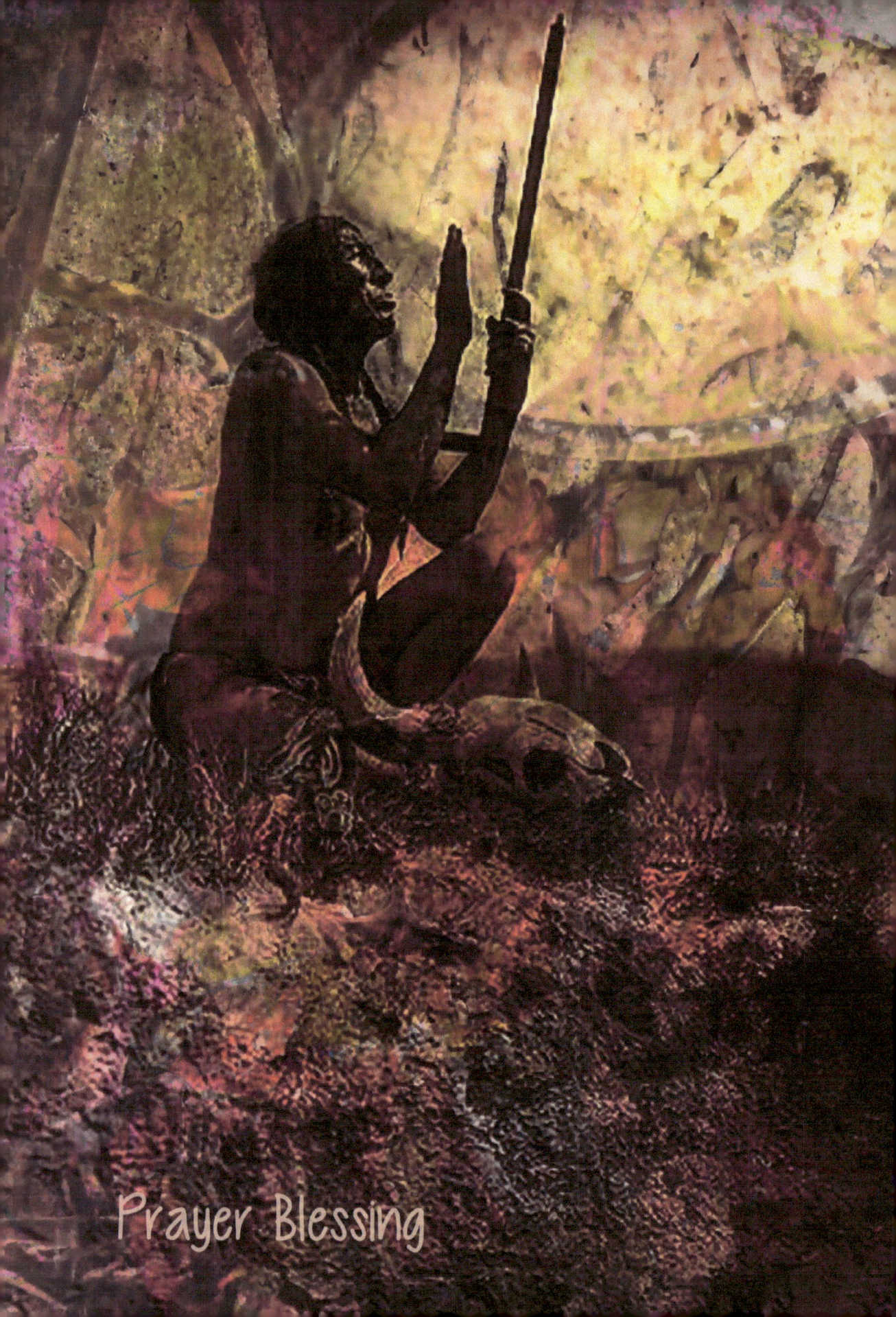

Prayer Blessing

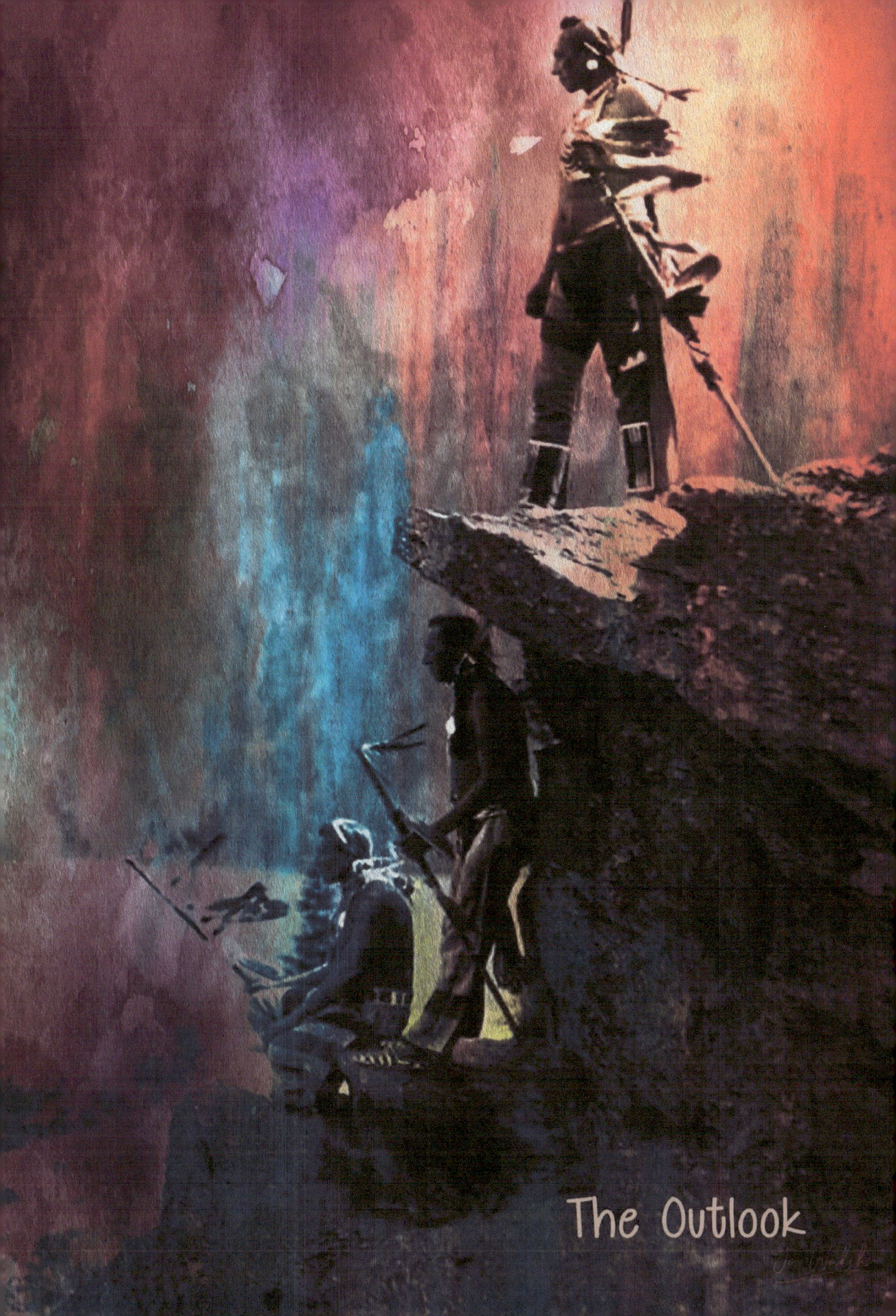

The Outlook

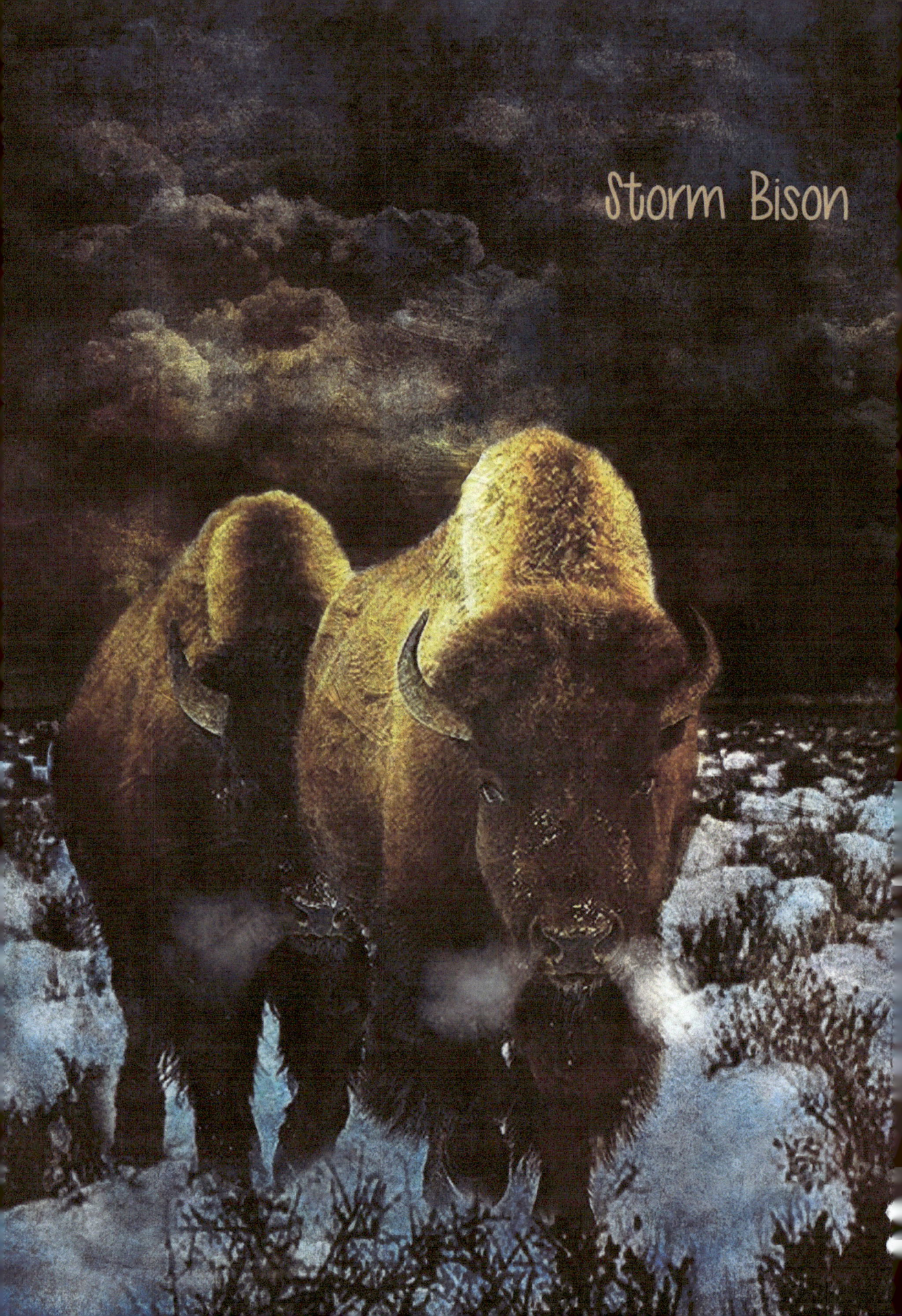

Storm Bison

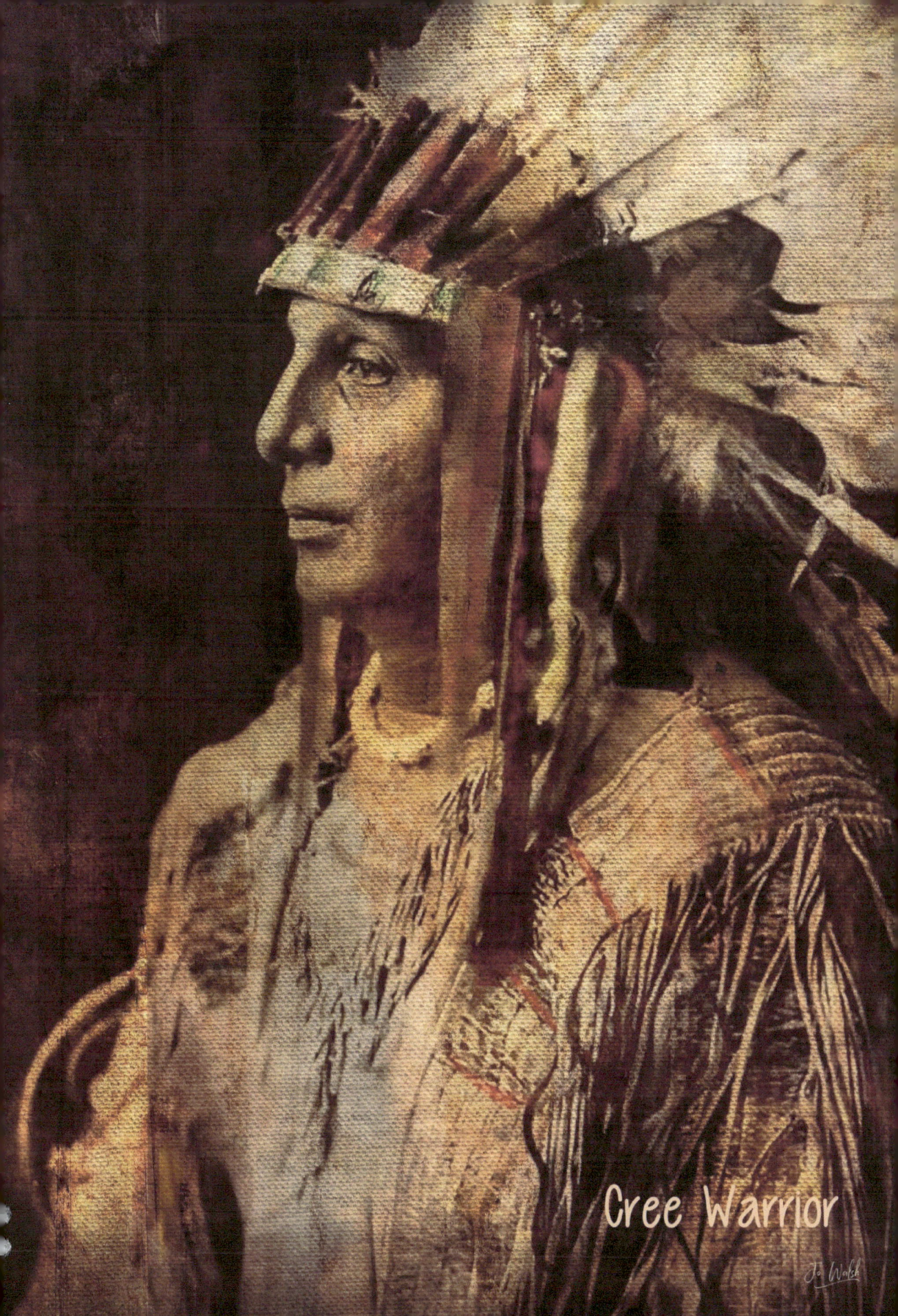

Cree Warrior

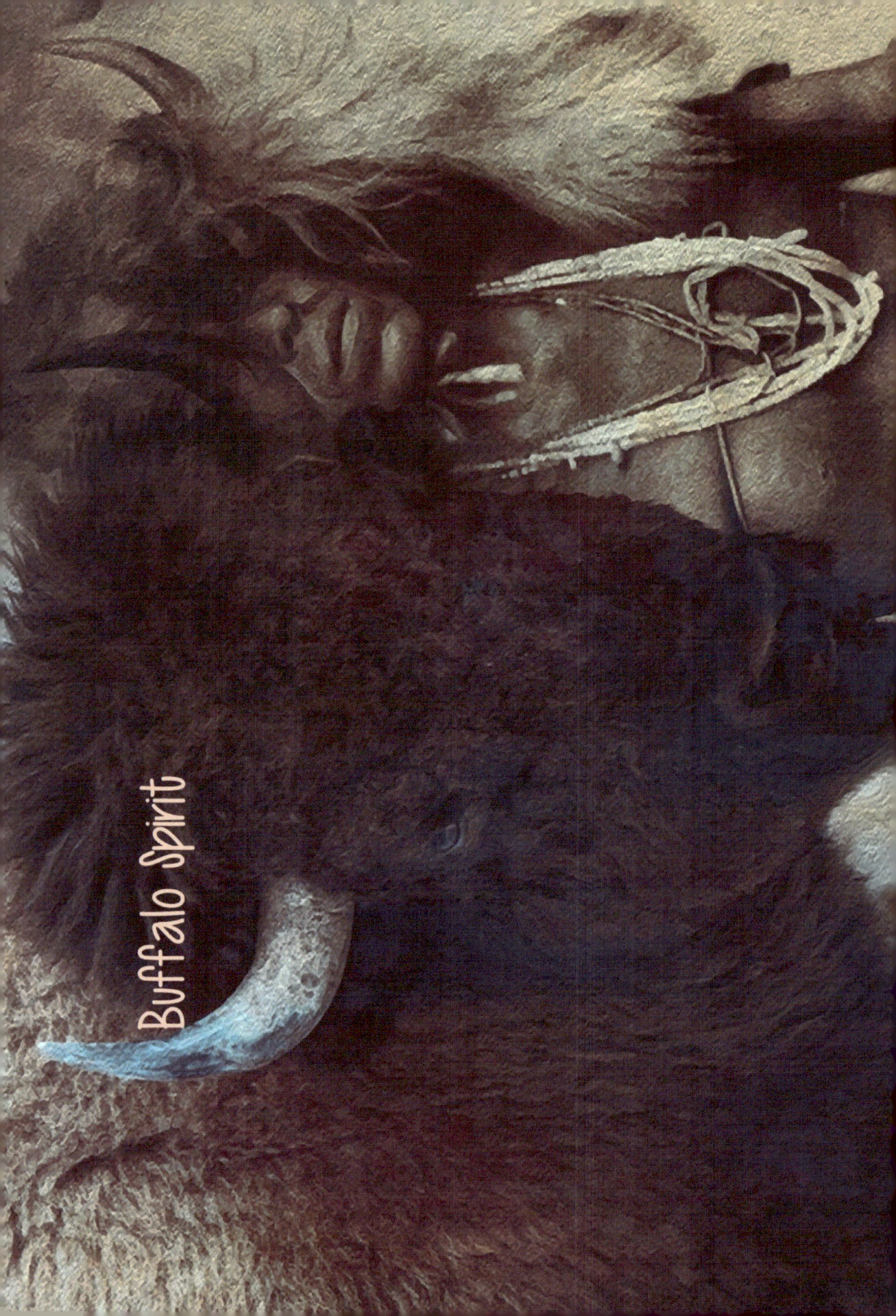

Buffalo Spirit

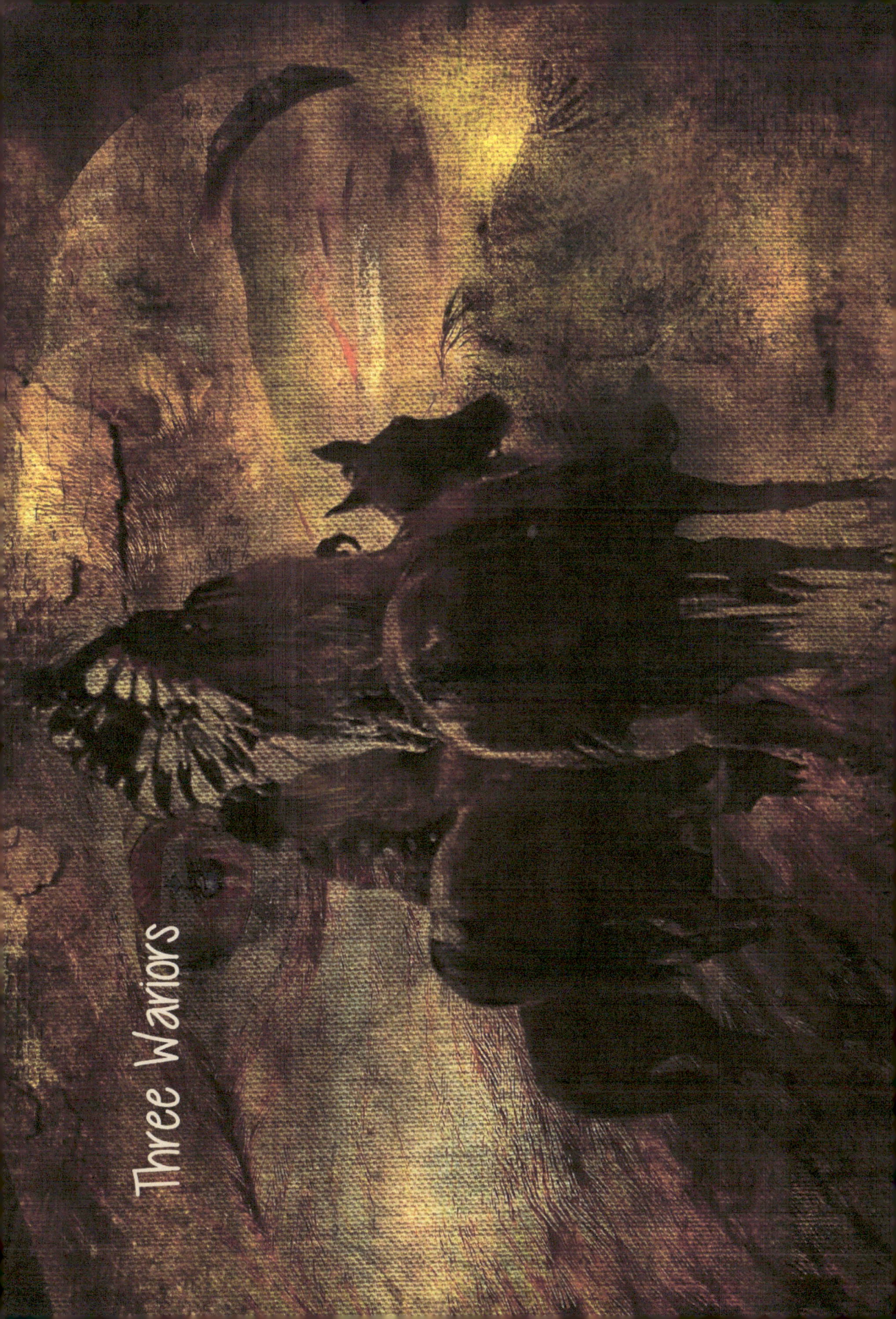

Three Warriors

Bear's Belly

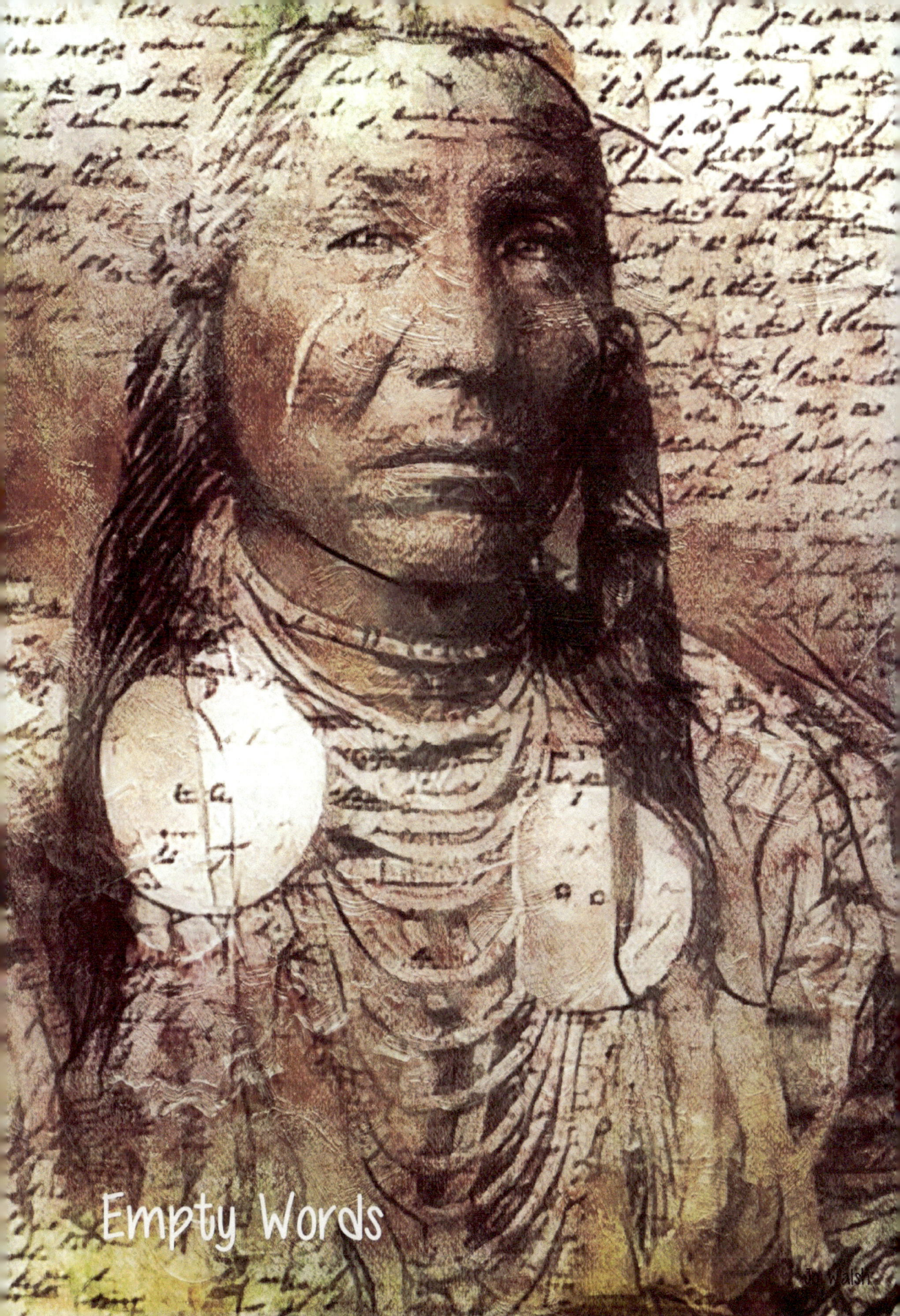

Empty Words

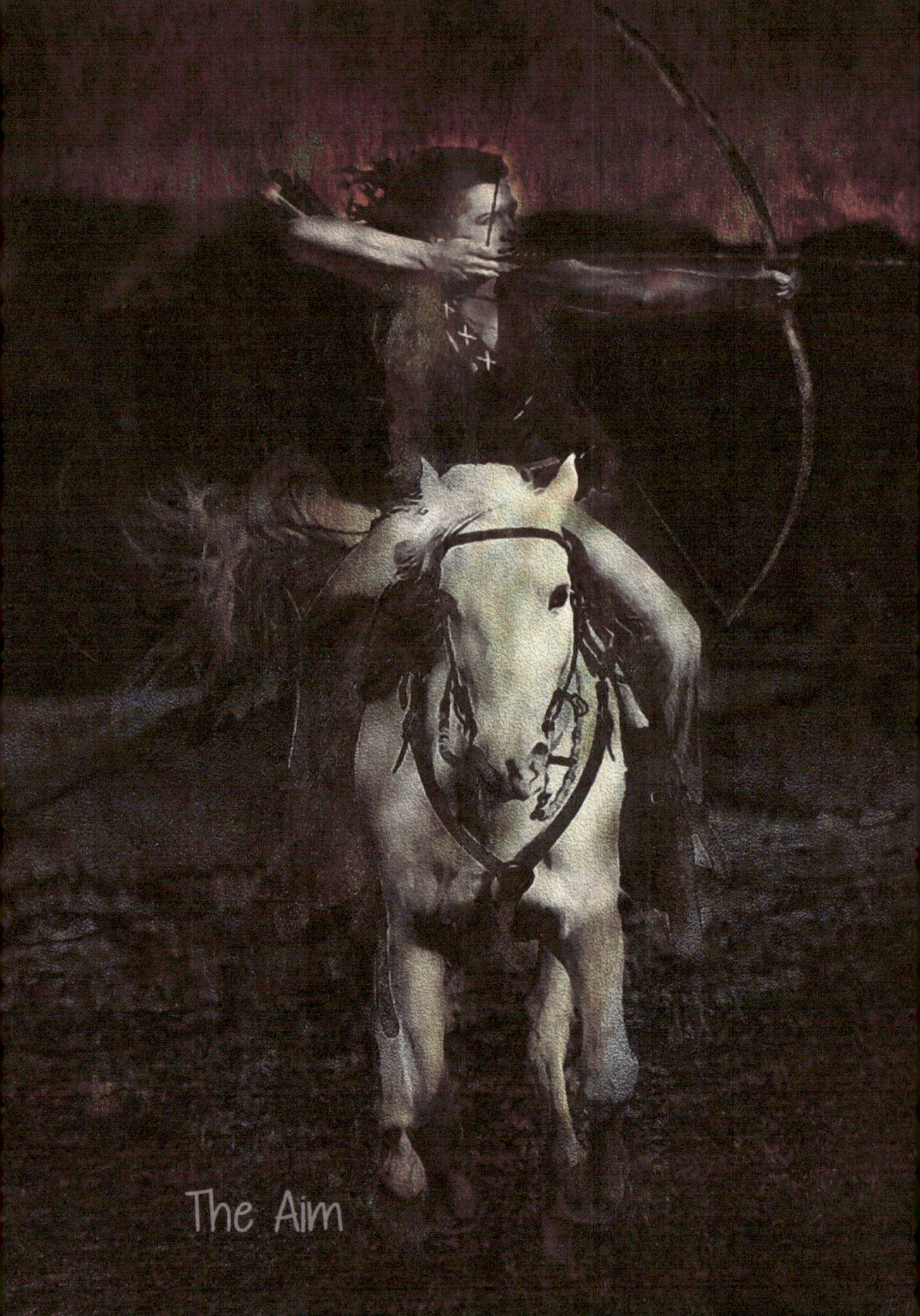

The Aim

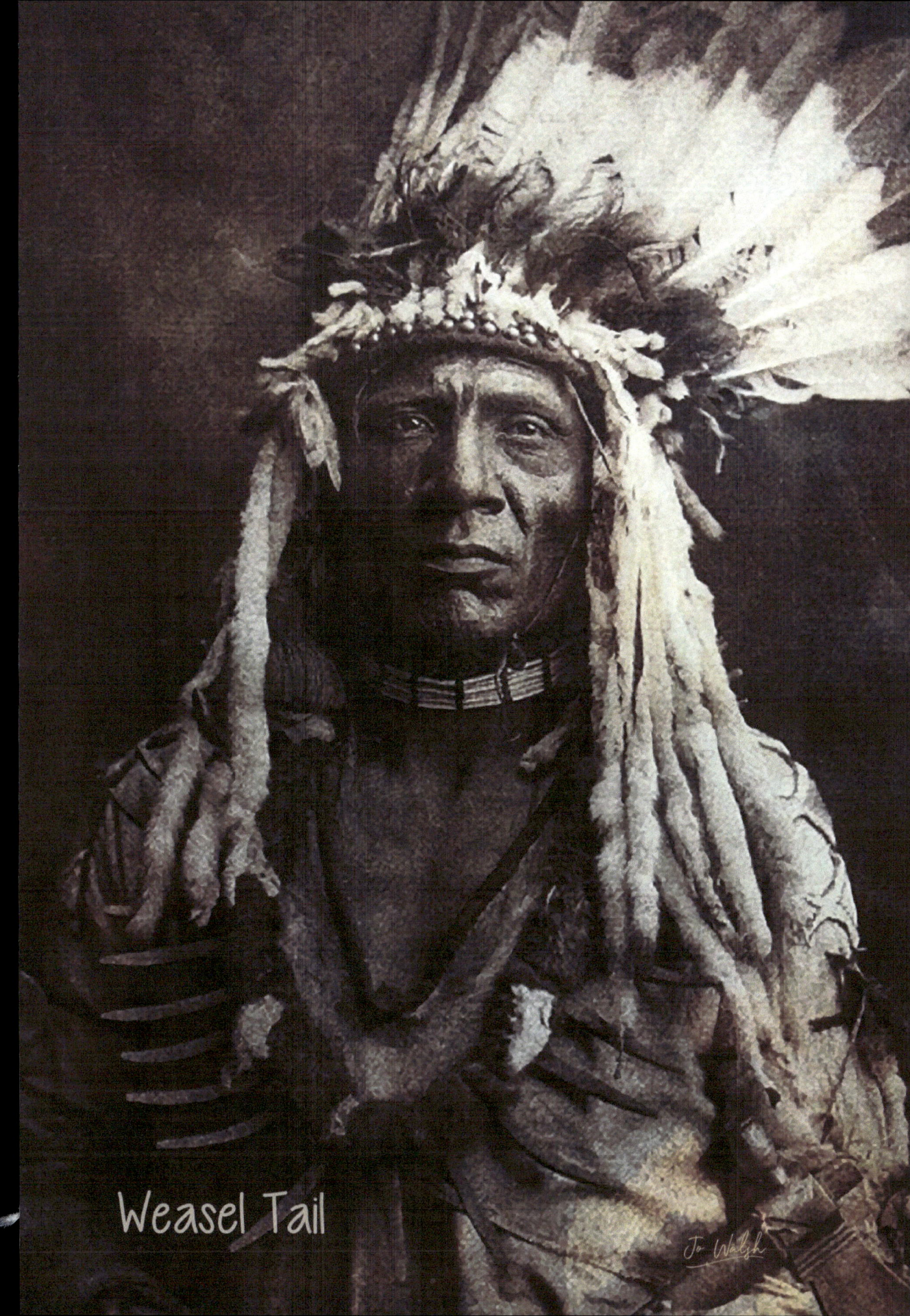

Weasel Tail

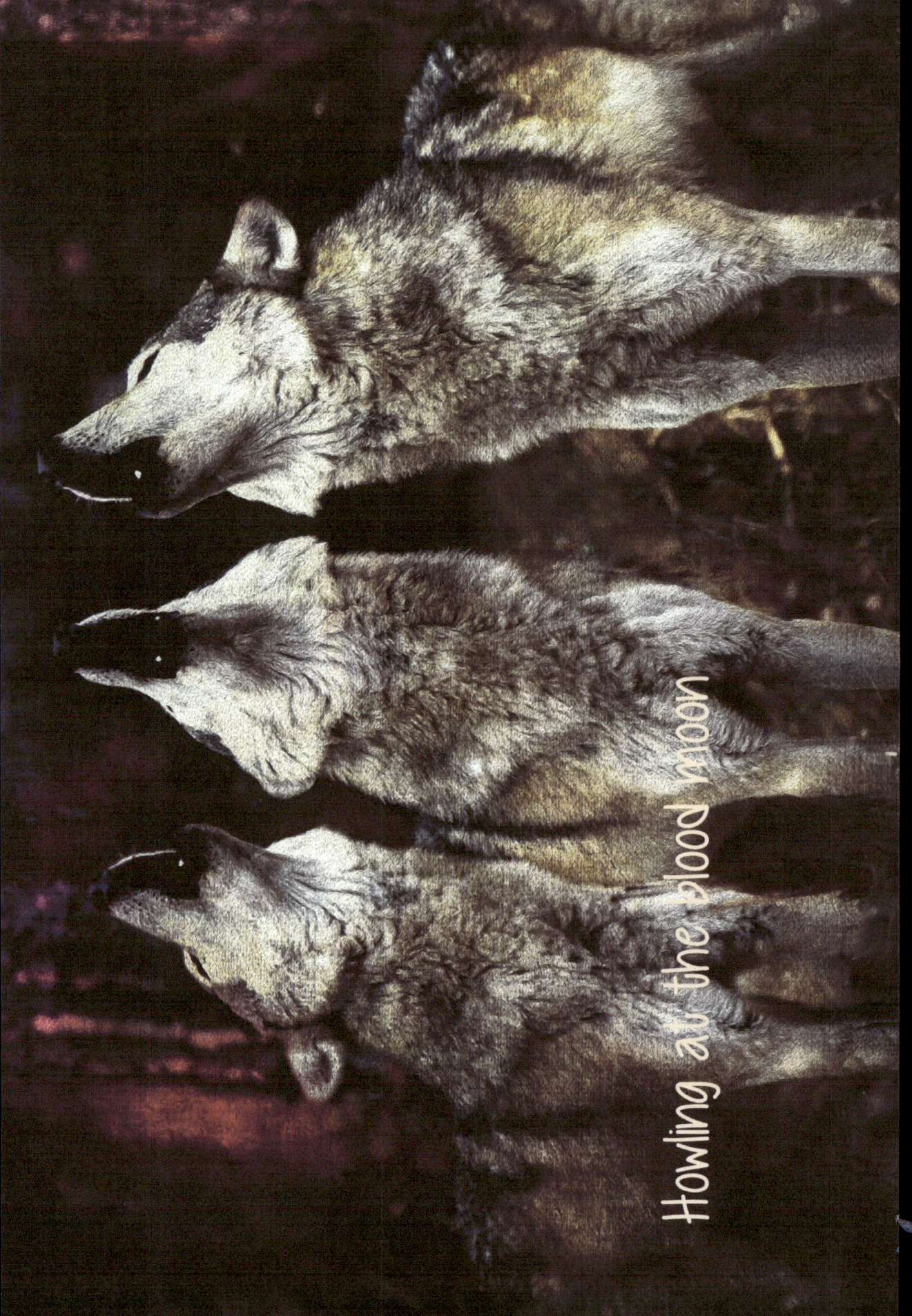

Howling at the blood moon

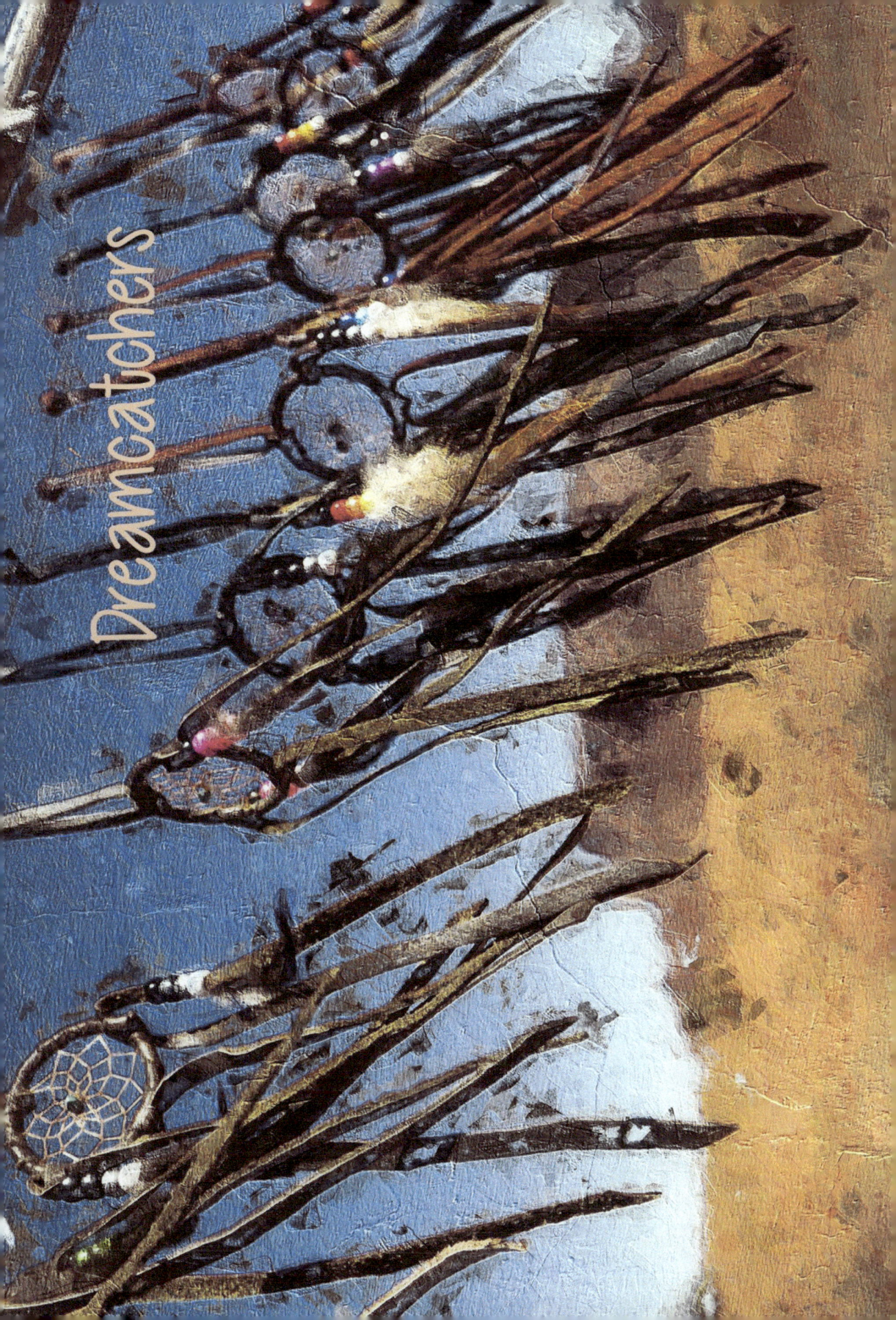

Dreamcatchers

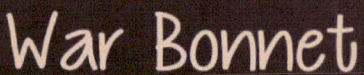

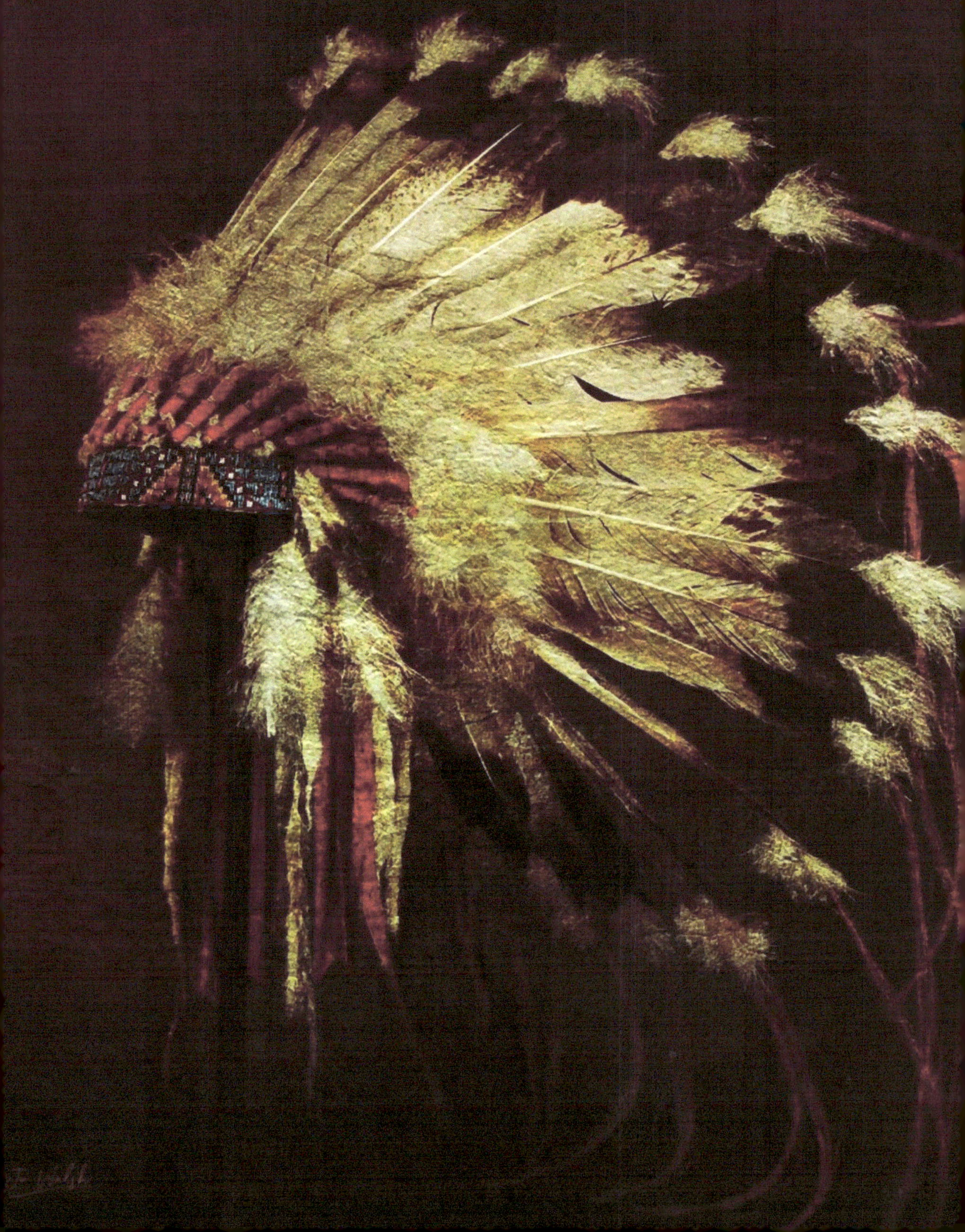

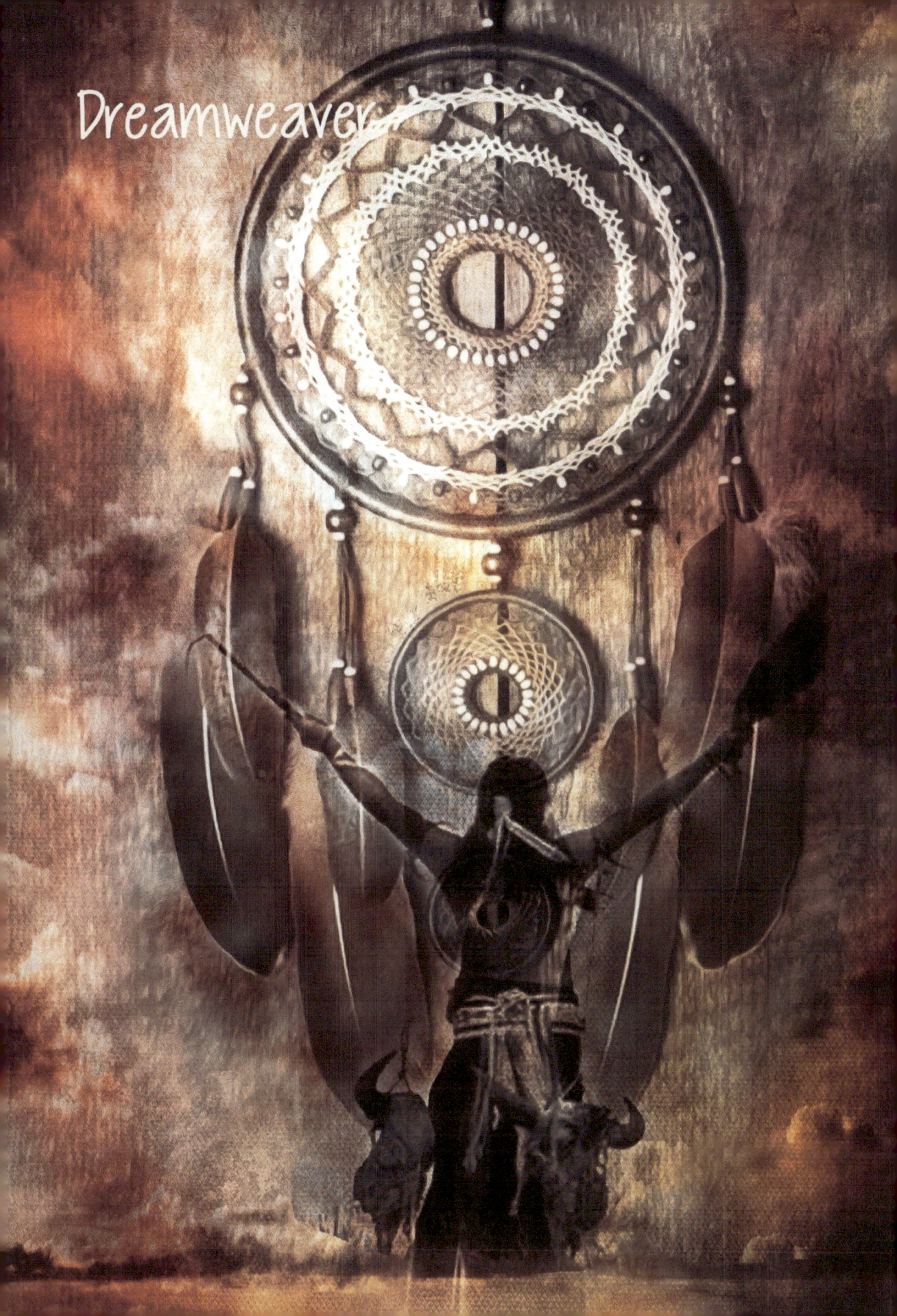

Dreamweaver

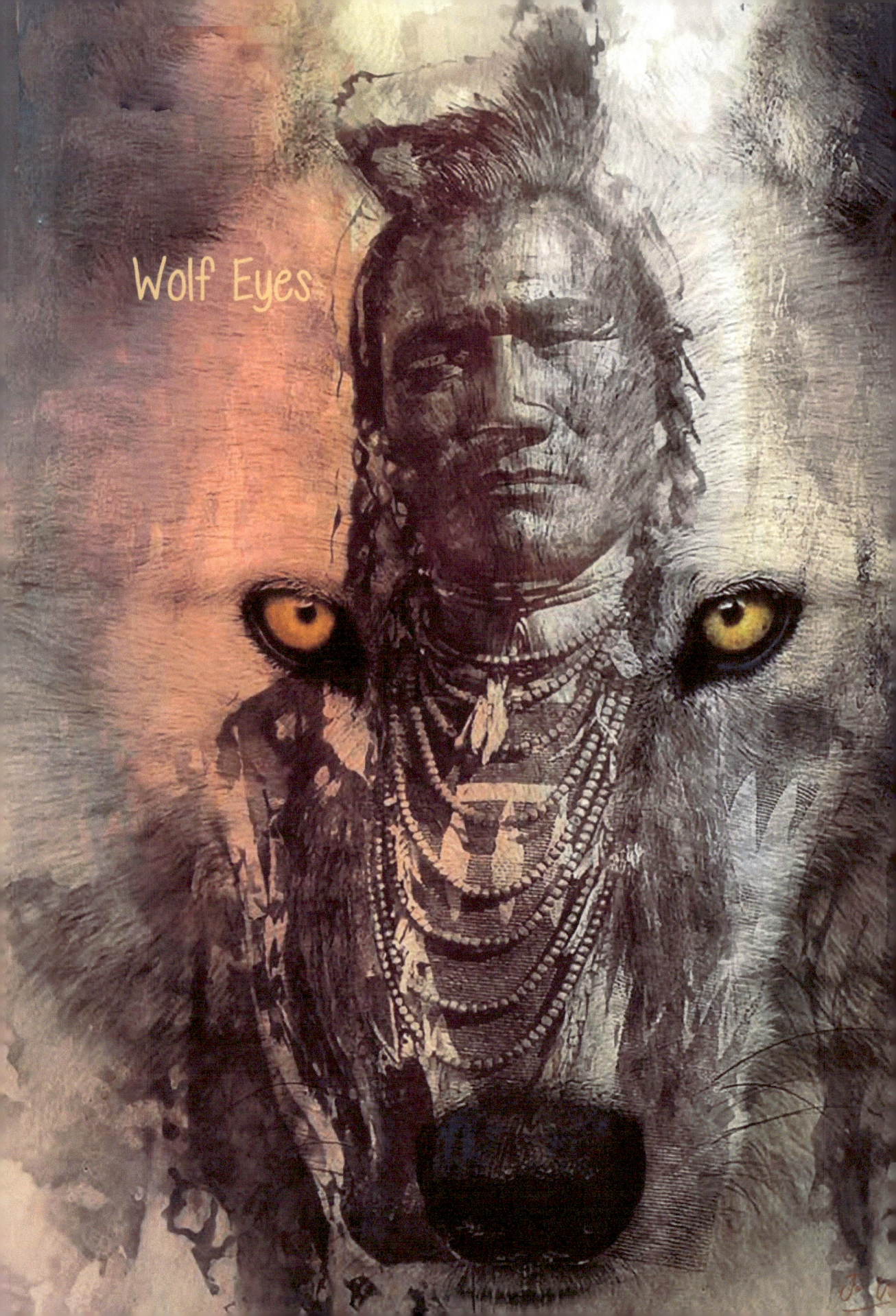
Wolf Eyes

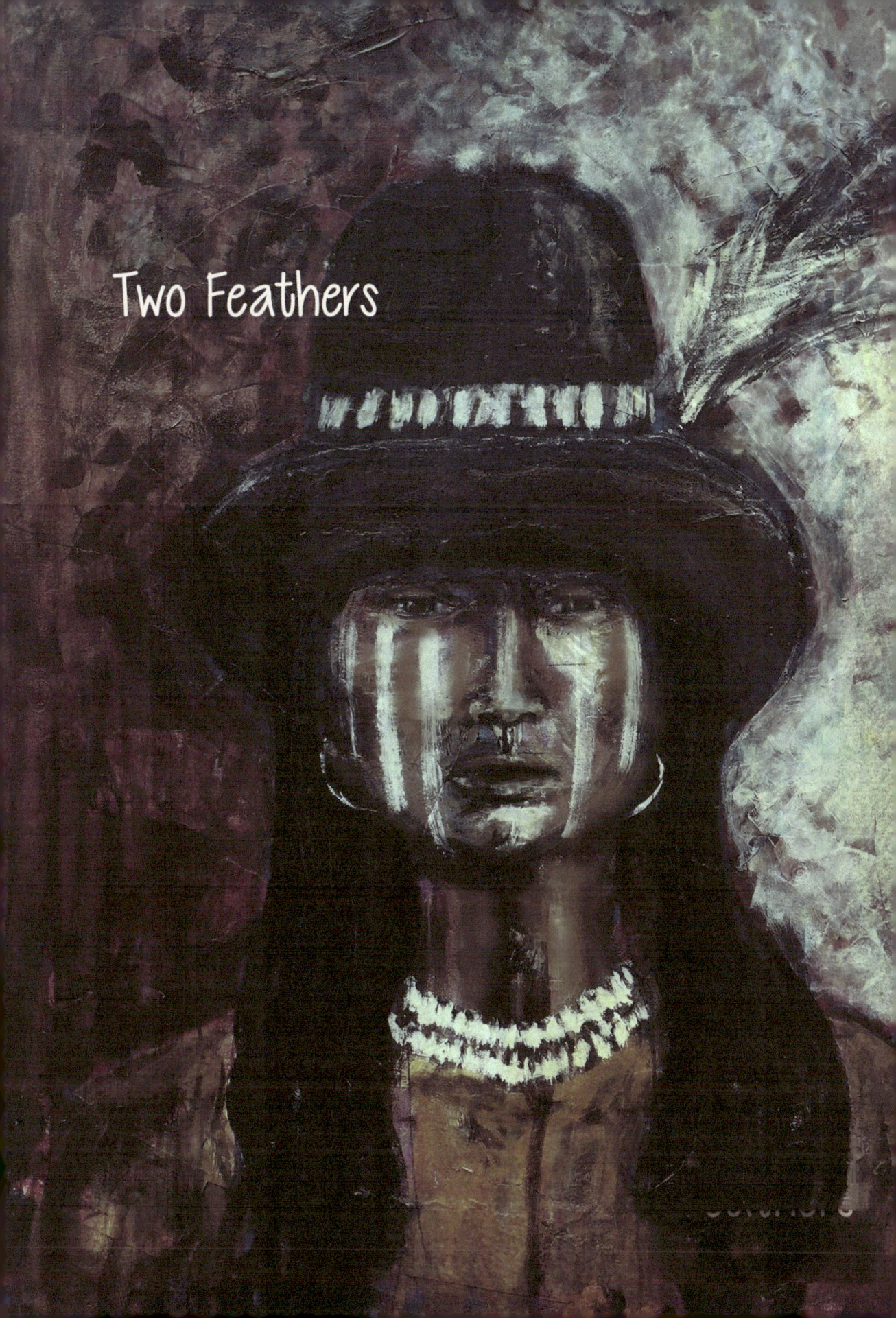

Two Feathers

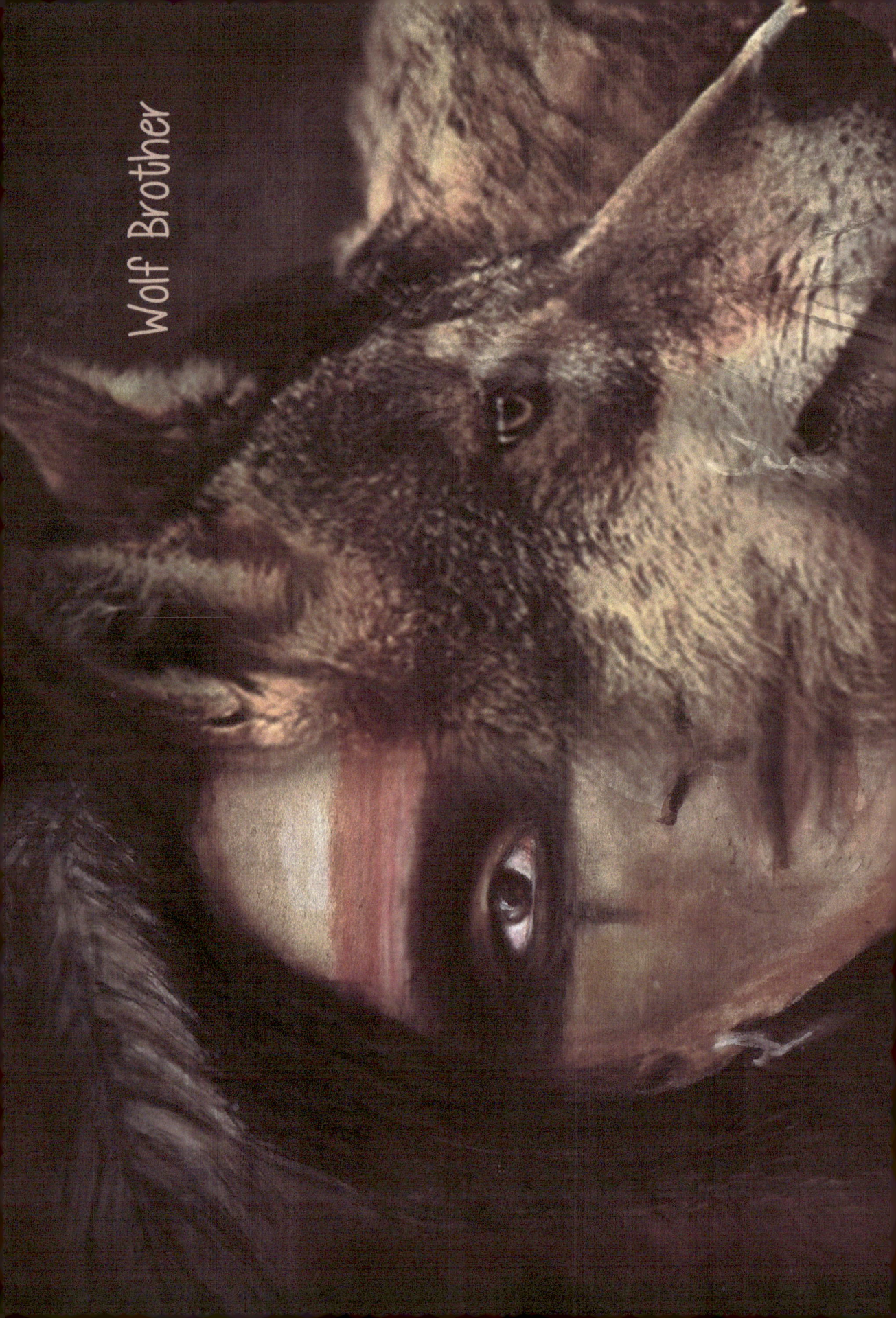

Wolf Brother

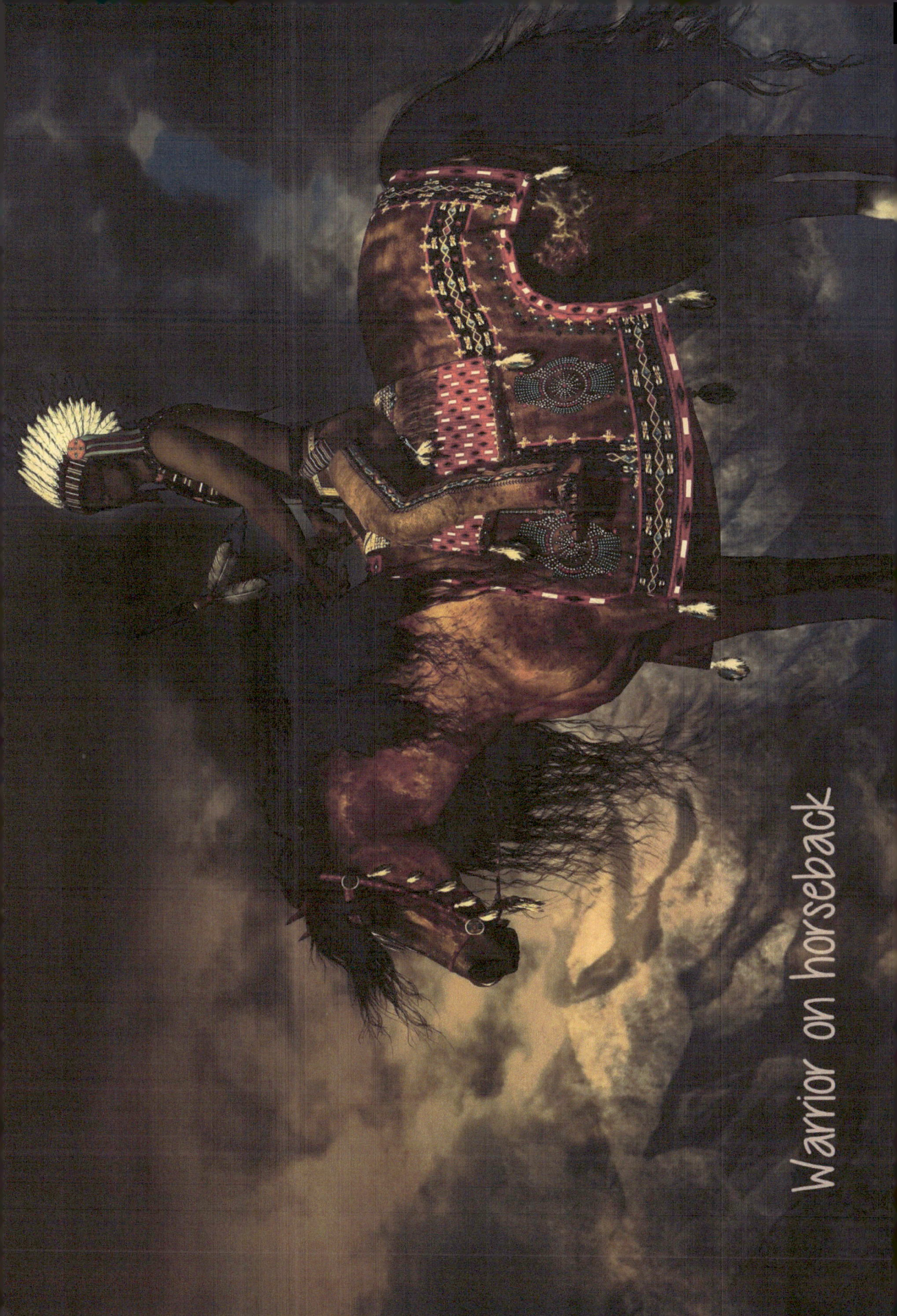

Warrior on horseback

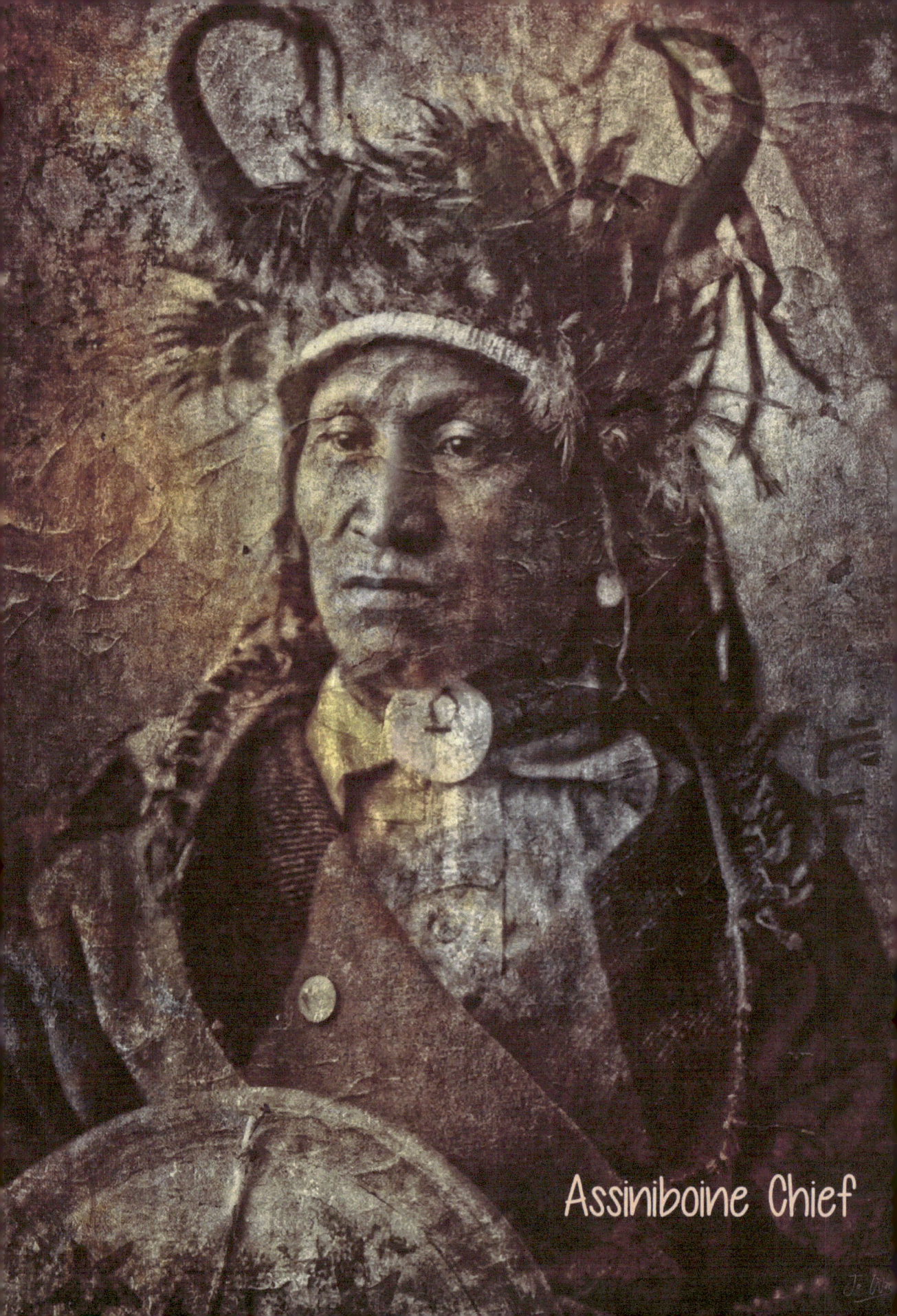

Assiniboine Chief

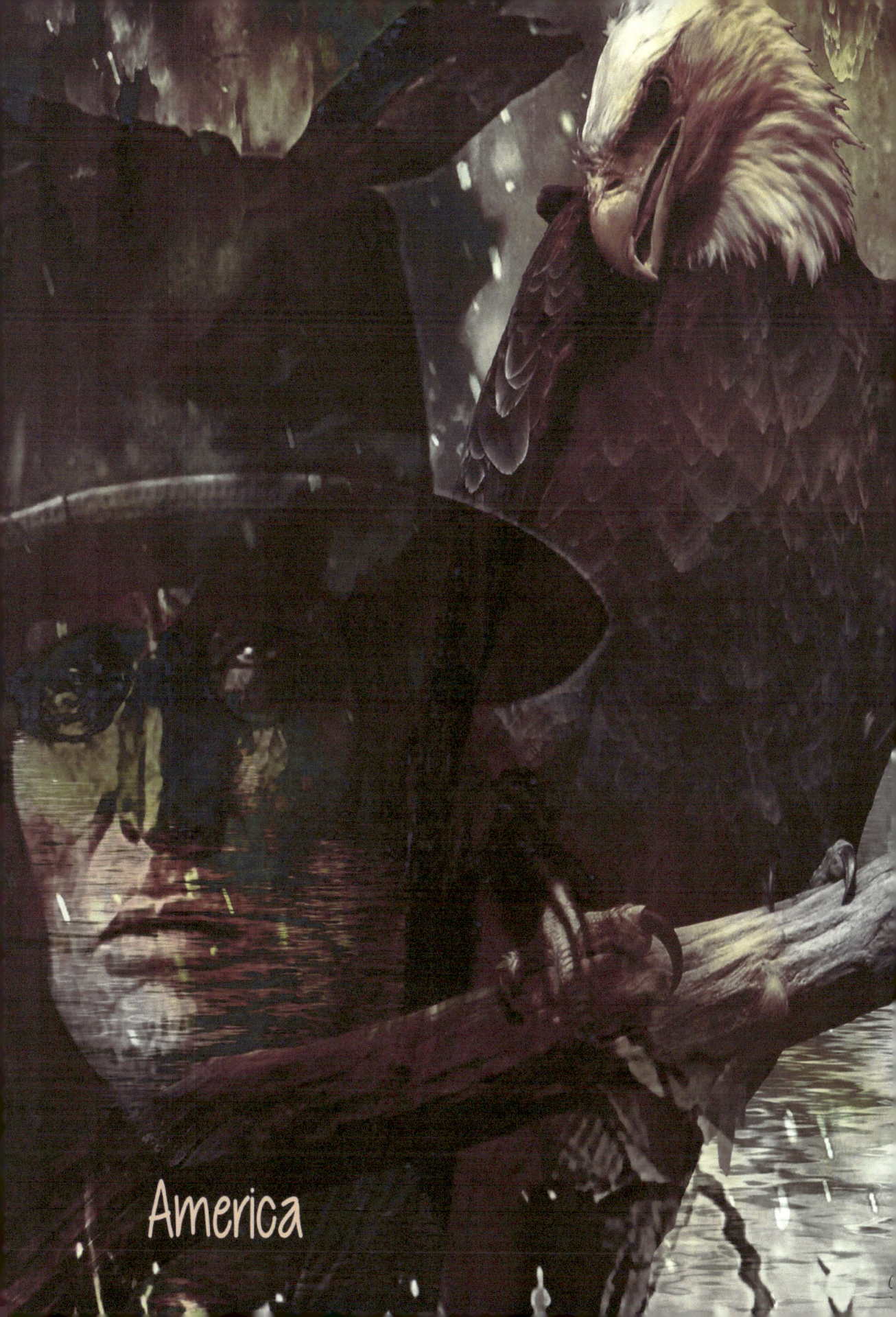

America

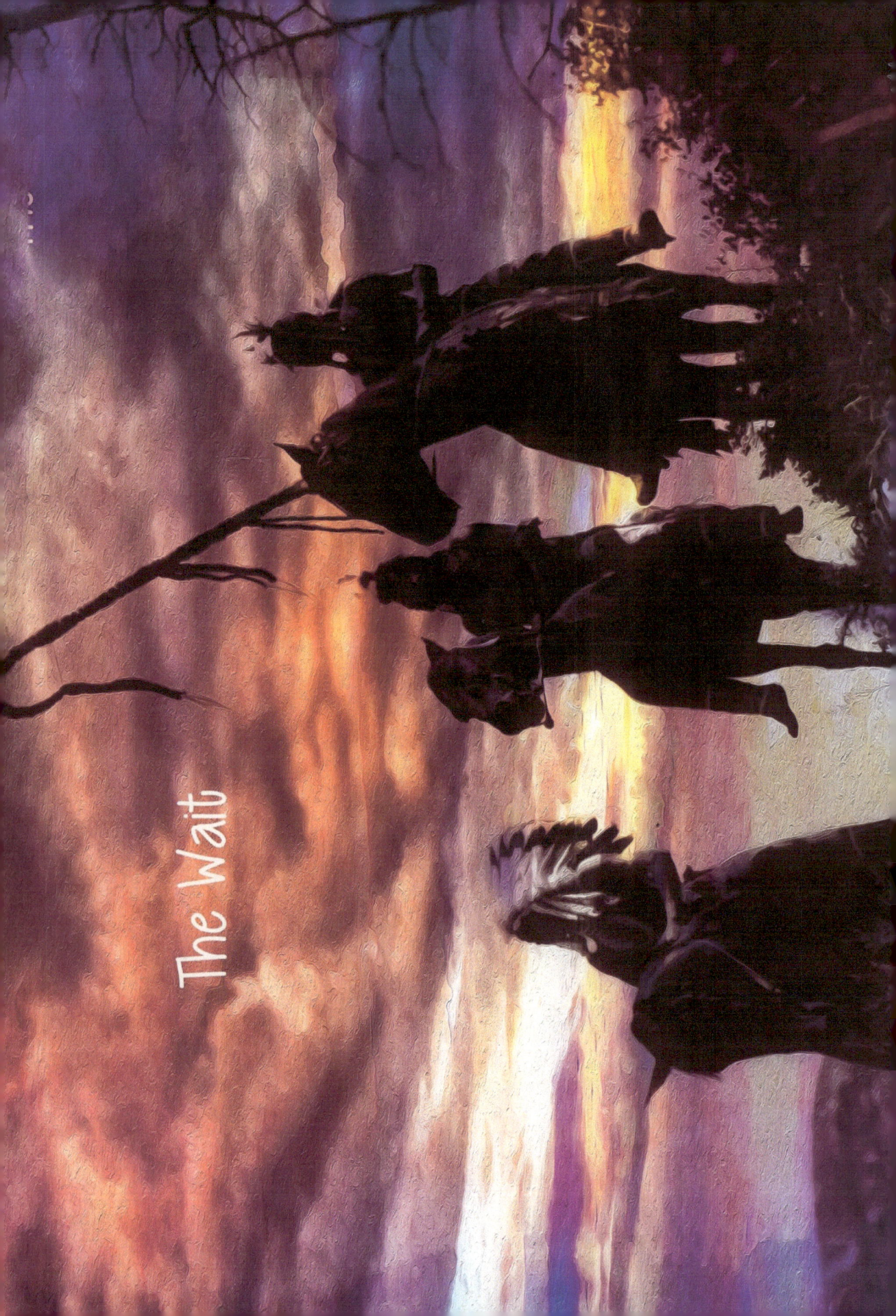

The Wait

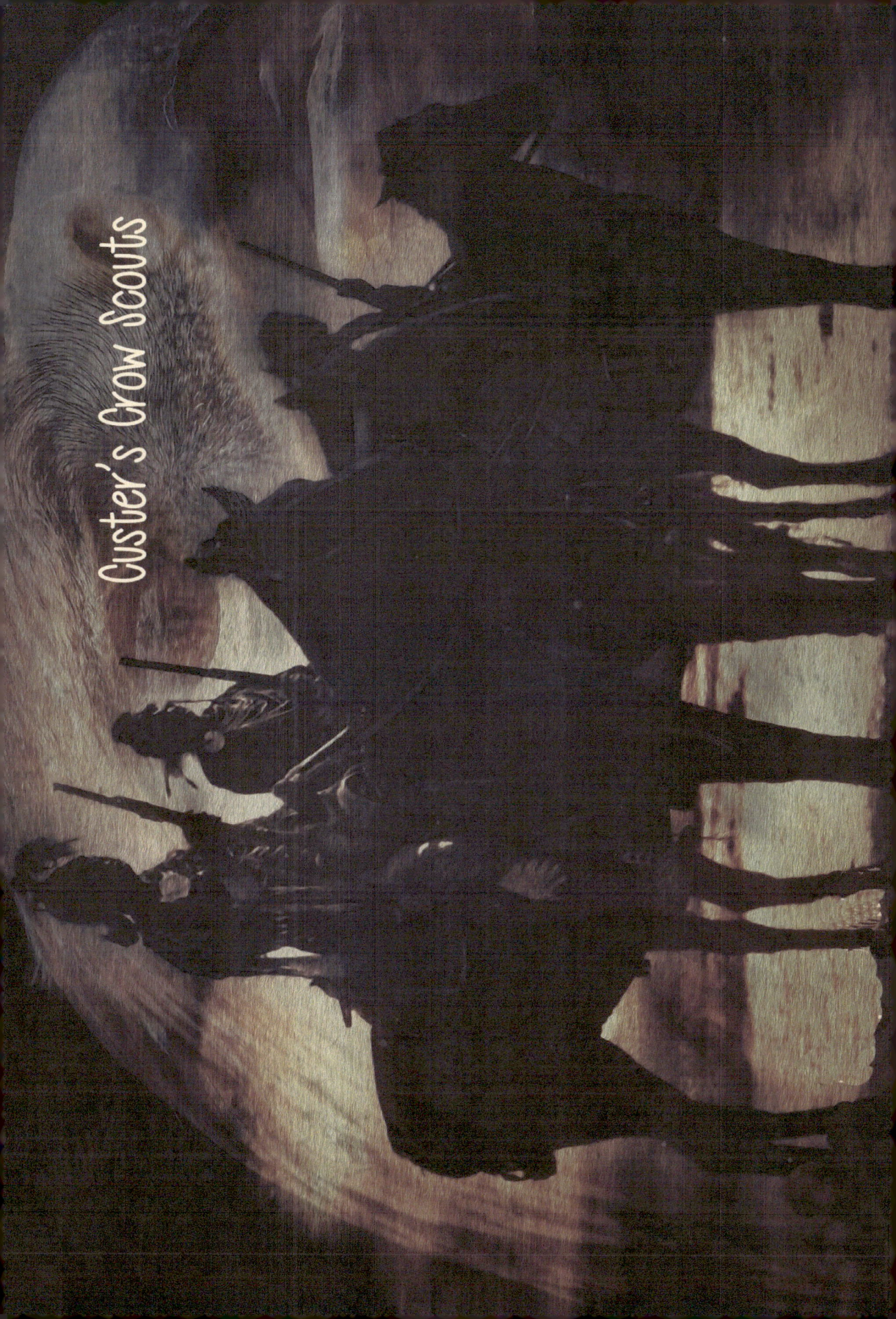

Custer's Crow Scouts

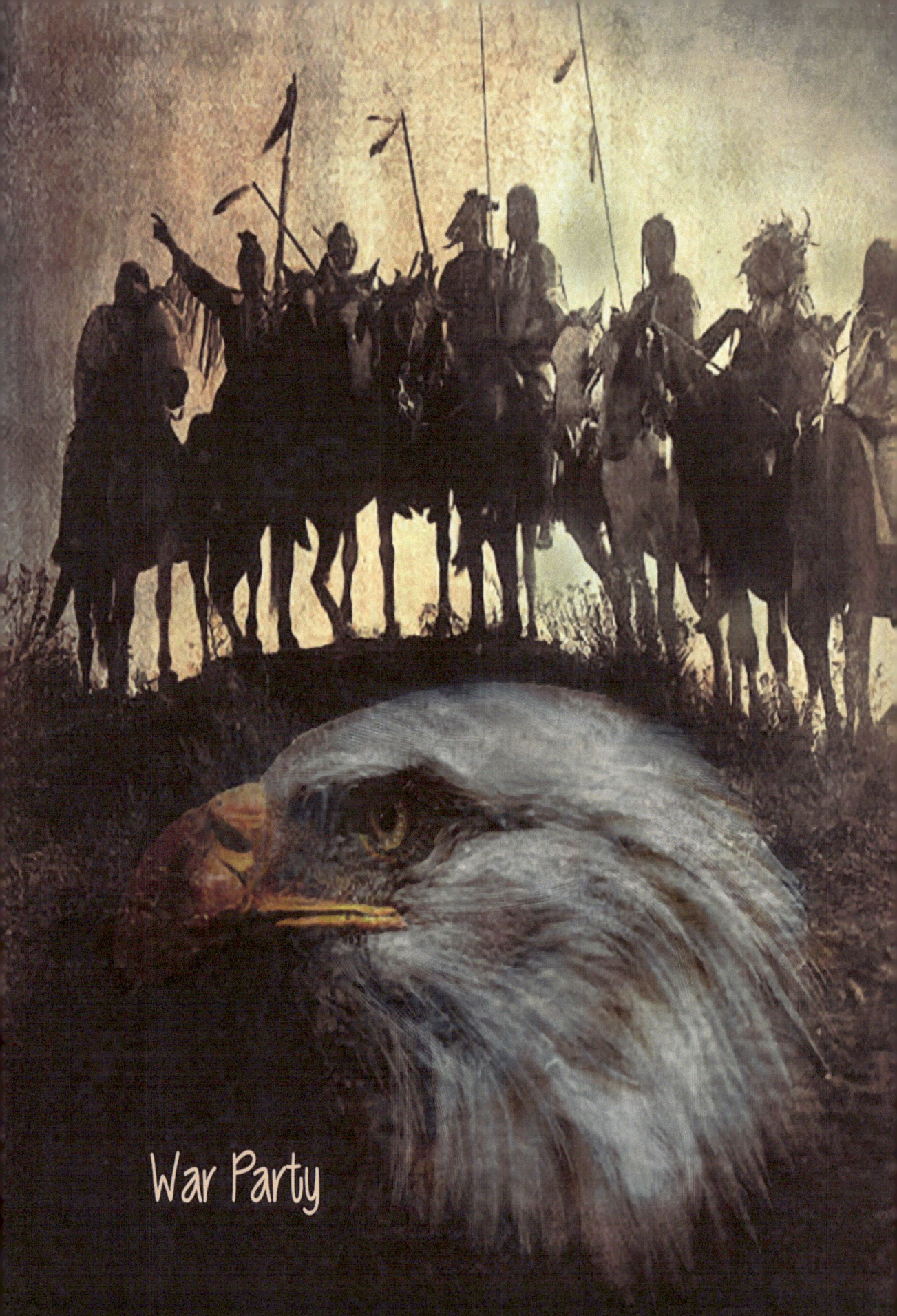

War Party

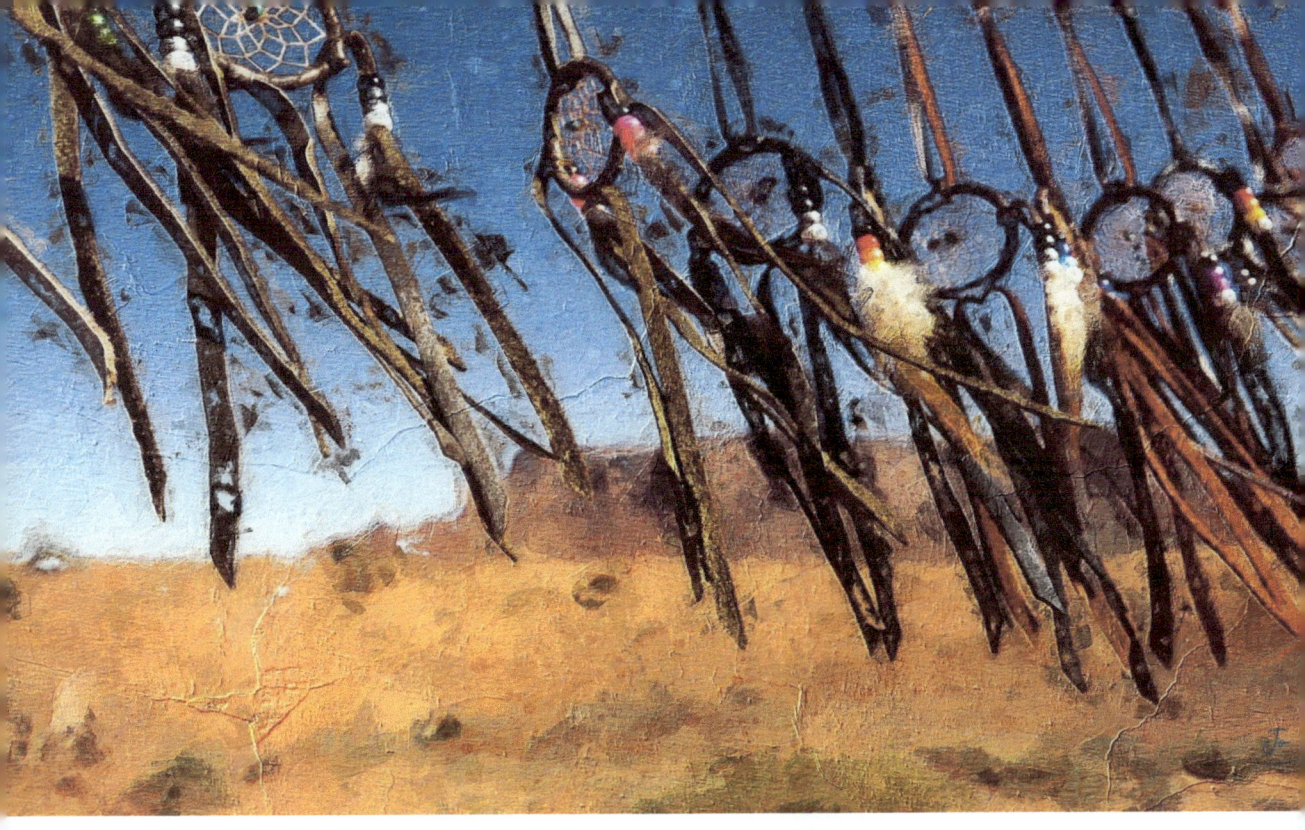

TRIBALSPIRITSART.COM

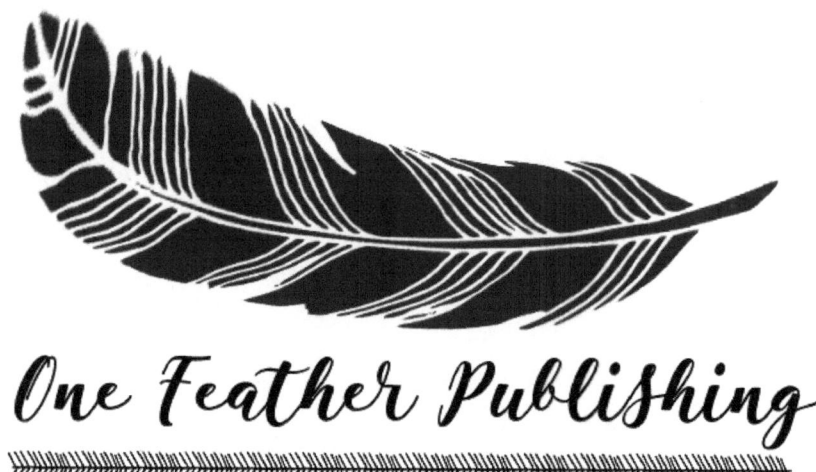

One Feather Publishing